RECORD BREAKERS

Machines and Inventions

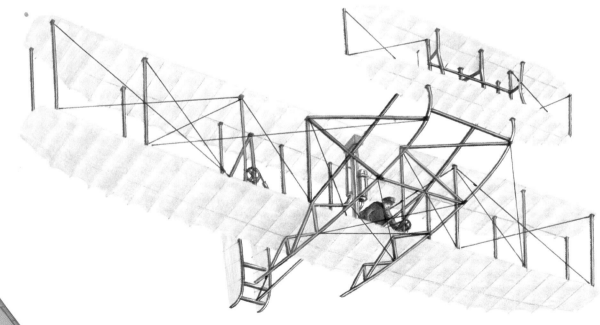

Written by Peter Lafferty

WATTS BOOKS

London • New York • Sydney

CONTENTS

First published in 1994 by
Watts Books
96 Leonard Street
London EC2A 4RH

© 1994 Orpheus Books Ltd

Illustrations by Sebastian Quigley
(Linden Artists), Alan Weston
(Kathy Jakeman Illustration), Roger
Stewart, Martin Woodward

Text consultant: Dr Trevor
Williams

Created and produced by
Nicholas Harris and Joanna
Turner, Orpheus Books Ltd

ISBN 0 7496 1819 1

A CIP record for this book is available from
the British Library.

Printed and bound in England

Picture acknowledgements: 8tr Science
Photo Library; 8cl Harry Ransom
Humanities Research Center, The
University of Texas at Austin; 8c Société
Française de Photographie; 9l Gilman
Paper Company Collection, New York; 9c
Science Museum; 9r Royal Photographic
Society; 31 Hulton-Deutsch Collection

INTRODUCTION

IN 1987 A TRAIN CARRIED PASSENGERS at 400 km/h – a world record speed. Yet the train never touched the track as it hurtled along: it was supported in the air by a magnetic field. Meanwhile, the US space probe Pioneer 10, launched back in 1972 on a journey to take photographs of Jupiter, has now left the Solar System and is more than 8000 million kilometres from Earth. It is the remotest man-made object. A little closer to our planet, the Hubble Space Telescope is sending back detailed pictures of galaxies thousands of billions of kilometres distant. It is so powerful it could detect light shone from a small torch 400,000 kilometres away!

As modern technology advances, more and more astonishing records like these will be broken. The first machines would have seemed just as impressive to people hundreds of years ago. The first passenger-carrying vehicle, a steam-powered wagon built in 1769, reached the grand speed of 3 km/h, but still managed to take part in the world's first traffic accident when it crashed into a wall!

This book is the story of the record makers and breakers, past and present. It is both a log of their extraordinary achievements and a fascinating picture of superlative technology.

THE FIRST MECHANICAL CLOCK
AND OTHER GREAT CHINESE INVENTIONS

IF YOU GO OUT and buy this book with paper money, if you put up an umbrella, strike a match, fly a kite or push a wheelbarrow, you have the Chinese to thank. These things are so familiar to us today we scarcely wonder where they came from. But it was the Chinese who first invented them.

The iron plough, steel manufacturing, printing, the rocket and many more important inventions were all thought up by the Chinese many centuries before they appeared in the West. The mechanical clock (see opposite), magnetic compass, suspension bridge, playing cards, parachute, paddle-wheel boats, even the decimal system – all first appeared in China.

Some of these inventions found their way to Europe through reports from travellers, while others were later 'invented' by Europeans unaware that they were already in existence. Without inventions that had had their origins in China, Europe in the Middle Ages might have been a very different place. Seed drills, iron ploughs, collar harnesses and the technique of growing crops in rows – ideas imported to Europe from China – helped farmers. The magnetic compass, the ship's rudder, and other nautical improvements guided European explorers across the world's oceans in the 15th century. Gunpowder greatly strenghtened armies. Printing presses spread learning around the world.

From late medieval times, far fewer inventions came out of China. Since then, most technological advances have been made in Europe, North America or Japan.

The first machine to record earthquakes, called a *seismograph*, was invented in AD 132. When it is shaken, a rod inside the machine swings and opens one of eight dragons' jaws. A ball drops into the toad's mouth below, recording the direction of the earthquake.

Invented in the first century BC, the Chinese wheelbarrow needs much less effort to move it than modern designs. The weight is balanced evenly on either side of the wheel.

GREAT CHINESE FIRSTS

Magnetic compass **4th century** BC
  Known in Europe 11th century
Paper **2nd century** BC *First paper made in Europe in 12th century*
Rudder **1st century** AD *Adopted by Europeans in about 1180*
Suspension bridge **1st century** AD *Suspension bridge built in United States 1801*
Fishing-reel **3rd century** AD *Known in Europe 17th century*
Umbrella **4th century** AD *Known in Europe 18th century*
Matches **6th century** AD *Made in Europe 19th century*
Printing **8th century** AD *First European presses in 14th century*
Playing-cards **9th century** AD *Known in Europe 13th century*
Paper money **9th century** AD *Made in Sweden in 1661*
Gunpowder **9th century** AD *Used in Europe 13th century*
Rocket **12th century** AD *Made in Europe 14th century*

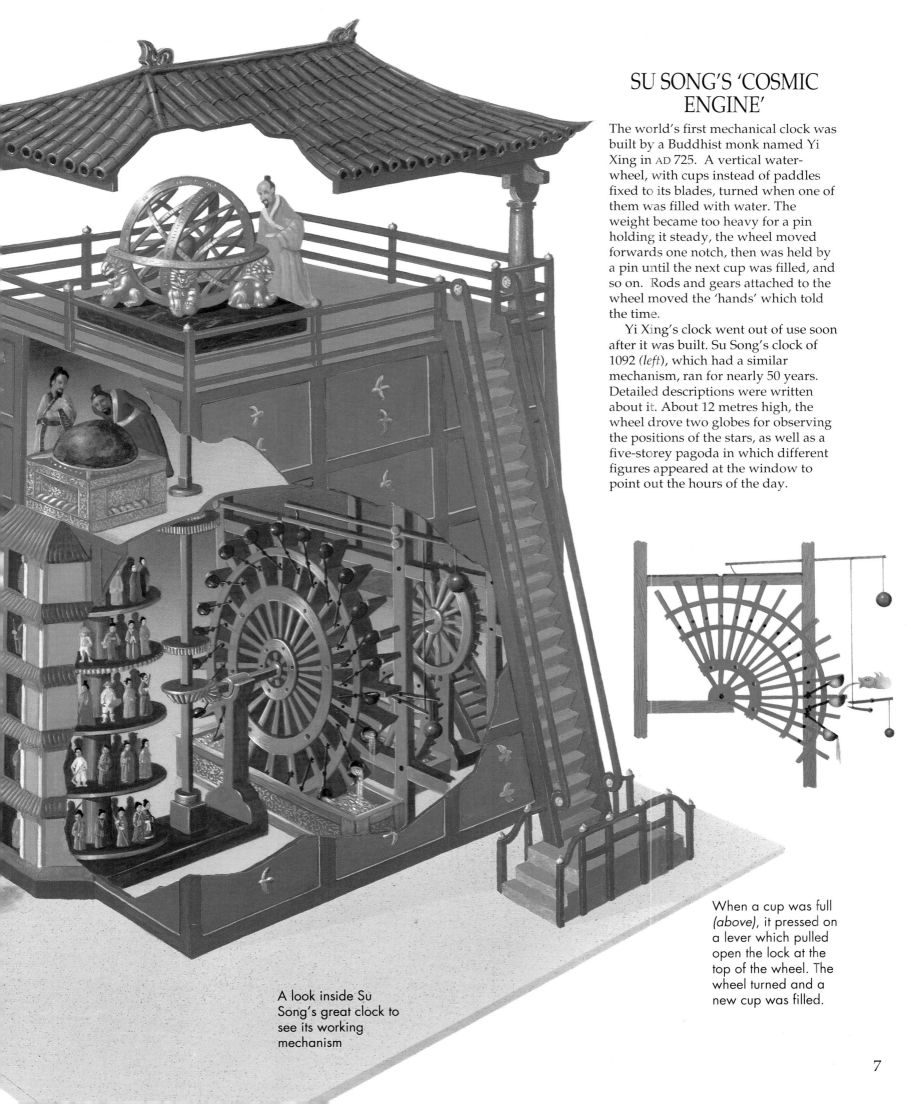

SU SONG'S 'COSMIC ENGINE'

The world's first mechanical clock was built by a Buddhist monk named Yi Xing in AD 725. A vertical water-wheel, with cups instead of paddles fixed to its blades, turned when one of them was filled with water. The weight became too heavy for a pin holding it steady, the wheel moved forwards one notch, then was held by a pin until the next cup was filled, and so on. Rods and gears attached to the wheel moved the 'hands' which told the time.

Yi Xing's clock went out of use soon after it was built. Su Song's clock of 1092 (left), which had a similar mechanism, ran for nearly 50 years. Detailed descriptions were written about it. About 12 metres high, the wheel drove two globes for observing the positions of the stars, as well as a five-storey pagoda in which different figures appeared at the window to point out the hours of the day.

When a cup was full (above), it pressed on a lever which pulled open the lock at the top of the wheel. The wheel turned and a new cup was filled.

A look inside Su Song's great clock to see its working mechanism

THE FIRST PHOTOGRAPH

NIÉPCE'S HISTORIC IMAGE

THE EARLIEST PHOTOGRAPH that survives today was taken in 1827 by a Frenchman Joseph Nicéphore Niépce. Simple cameras, in which rays of light reflected from an object passed through a pinhole in a dark box to make an upside-down image on a screen inside, had been invented centuries earlier. The problem was how to make the image permanent. Niépce solved it by fitting his camera with a metal plate coated with a thin layer of bitumen (the substance used to surface roads) and oil. After eight hours, a ghostly image formed on the plate. The quality of photographic images was soon improved by another Frenchman, Louis Daguerre, and an Englishman, William Fox Talbot.

X-rays were discovered – accidentally – by German scientist Wilhelm Röntgen in 1895. These invisible rays can pass through many materials, such as flesh, but not through metal or bone. Röntgen made the first X-ray photograph *(right)* of his wife's hand in 1896. Her ring is clearly visible.

Daguerre's photograph of an artist's studio, the world's first fully successful photograph (1837). It was called a daguerrotype, a photograph on a copper plate fixed with ordinary salt.

The earliest surviving photograph was a view taken in 1827 by Nicéphore Niépce from the window of his home at Chalon-sur-Saône, near Beaune, France.

American inventor George Eastman introduced the easy-to-use Kodak camera *(right)* in 1888 and photography soon became popular. Eastman also produced the first roll films.

THE FIRST MOVIES

In 1891 American inventor Thomas Alva Edison *(see page 10)* built a machine called the Kinetoscope. It was the first successful moving-picture machine, although only one person at a time could view through an eyepiece as the sequence of photographs on a strip of film wound past. Just four years later, two brothers, Auguste and Louis Lumière gave the first public cinema show in a cafe in Paris. The films showed scenes of everyday life in the city.

These five photographs *(below)* are milestones in the early history of photography.

Fox Talbot's 1835 photograph of a window at Lacock Abbey. It was the first photograph made by the negative-positive process, which allows many copies to be made.

The first colour photograph was made in 1861 by the Scottish physicist James Clerk Maxwell.

Frenchman Hippolyte Bayard discovered how to make positive images directly on paper. He took this photo of windmills in Montmartre, Paris, in 1839.

THE FASTEST CAMERA

The fastest production camera is the image converter, or Imacon camera. It is used in scientific and industrial research. The image converter camera can reveal what happens when a high-speed bullet hits a target, for example. Light entering the camera is converted into an electron beam (like the inside of a television camera tube). This forms an image that can be recorded on film. There is less than one billionth of a second between each image, which means that a sequence of a billion images could be taken in one second!

TALKING MACHINES

In March 1876, American inventor Alexander Graham Bell made the world's first telephone call. His assistant, Tom Watson, in the next room, heard the words "Mr Watson, come here, I want to see you." In Bell's telephone, there was a steel strip which vibrated when someone spoke close to it. These vibrations could be sent along a wire with an electric current and make another strip vibrate, reproducing the original sounds. These were not very clear: users of the first telephones had to shout to make themselves heard!

The telephone was improved by another American inventor, Thomas Alva Edison, so that it could be used over long distances. Some of its parts he also adapted to produce the first recording machine, which he called the phonograph. The first recorded sound was heard in 1877, when Edison listened to his own voice saying "Halloo, Halloo!"

His phonograph was like a telephone, only with the vibrating parts connected to a steel needle. As Edison spoke into a horn, the needle 'wrote' the pattern of vibrations on a piece of tinfoil wrapped round a drum, which was turned at the same time. When the needle was returned to the beginning of its written message and the drum turned again, the pattern cut in the foil made it vibrate in the same way. The telephone parts also vibrated and the sound came back out of the drum.

In this imaginary scene, five great inventors sit round a table, each with their famous inventions in front of them.

ALEXANDER GRAHAM BELL
First telephone (1876)

THOMAS EDISON
First recording machine (1877)

First electric light bulb (1879) (also invented by Joseph Swan)

GUGLIELMO MARCONI *(right)*
First radio transmission across Atlantic (1901)

MESSAGES WITHOUT WIRES

Radio waves, which carry radio sounds and television pictures, move through the air at the speed of light. Heinrich Hertz, a German physicist, sent the first radio signals over a short distance in 1887. Italian inventor Guglielmo Marconi showed that radio messages could be sent across the world. In 1901, Marconi sent the first transatlantic radio signal – the three dots of S in Morse code – from Cornwall, England, to Newfoundland in Canada, a distance of 3520 km.

FIRST WITH THE NEWS
GREAT ELECTRICAL INVENTIONS

THE TELEPHONE, television and radio are all so important to our daily lives it is difficult to imagine what we would do without them. Yet not much longer than 150 years ago, they did not even exist. The very first machine for sending messages was not electrical at all, but a tower with great mechanical arms fixed on top of it. The arms could be moved into different positions, each standing for a different word or number. Series of towers were built within sight of one another between two places, their operators relaying a message from one tower to the next. Called a semaphore telegraph, it first appeared in France in the 1790s.

*First electric telegraph
that recorded messages
on paper (1838)*

JOHN LOGIE BAIRD *(below, left)*
First television pictures (1926)

The Scottish inventor John Logie Baird was the first to give a demonstration of television in 1926. His camera used a spinning disc pierced with holes and an electronic 'eye'. The eye recorded the brightness of different parts of the image – the head of a ventriloquist's dummy – and transmitted what it 'saw' to a screen.

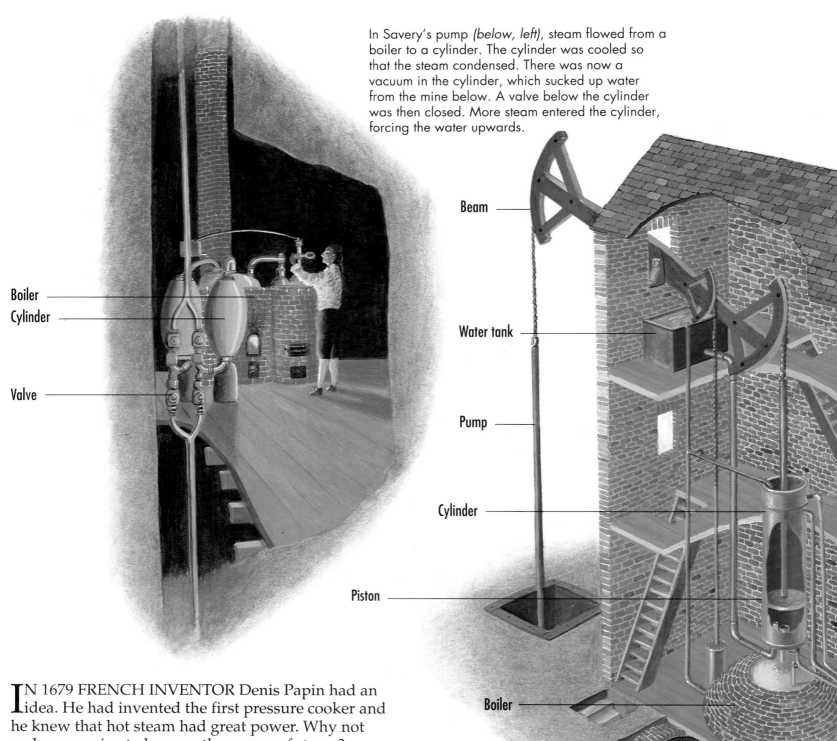

In Savery's pump *(below, left)*, steam flowed from a boiler to a cylinder. The cylinder was cooled so that the steam condensed. There was now a vacuum in the cylinder, which sucked up water from the mine below. A valve below the cylinder was then closed. More steam entered the cylinder, forcing the water upwards.

Boiler
Cylinder
Valve

Beam
Water tank
Pump
Cylinder
Piston
Boiler

IN 1679 FRENCH INVENTOR Denis Papin had an idea. He had invented the first pressure cooker and he knew that hot steam had great power. Why not make an engine to harness the power of steam? Unfortunately, Papin did not have the money to develop his idea. He died in poverty in 1714.

The first steam engine was designed in 1698 by Thomas Savery, an English engineer. It was called 'the miner's friend' because it was built to pump water out of mines. Its only known successful use, however, was in lifting water at large houses in London.

The first working steam engine was built in 1712 by the Cornish engineer Thomas Newcomen. A large beam rocked back and forth 16 times a minute as it pumped water. In 1776 James Watt, a Scottish instrument maker, improved the Newcomen engine. His engines did not waste as much heat and made better use of the power of steam.

For his engine *(above, right)*, Newcomen used atmospheric pressure not to suck up water but to drive down a piston. Steam was admitted to a cylinder at a pressure high enough to push up the piston inside it. The steam was then condensed by a spray of water, a vacuum was created, and atmospheric pressure drove the piston downwards. The movement of the piston rocked the beam back and forth and worked the pump.

THE FIRST STEAM ENGINES
DRIVING FORCE OF THE INDUSTRIAL REVOLUTION

Watt's engine *(below, right)* was the first really successful steam engine. Steam was condensed outside the main cylinder. This saved heat because the main cylinder never cooled down. Watt also used steam pressure to

force the piston down, rather than relying on atmospheric pressure. This increased the power of the engine. Wheels and belts linked the engine to spinning and weaving machines.

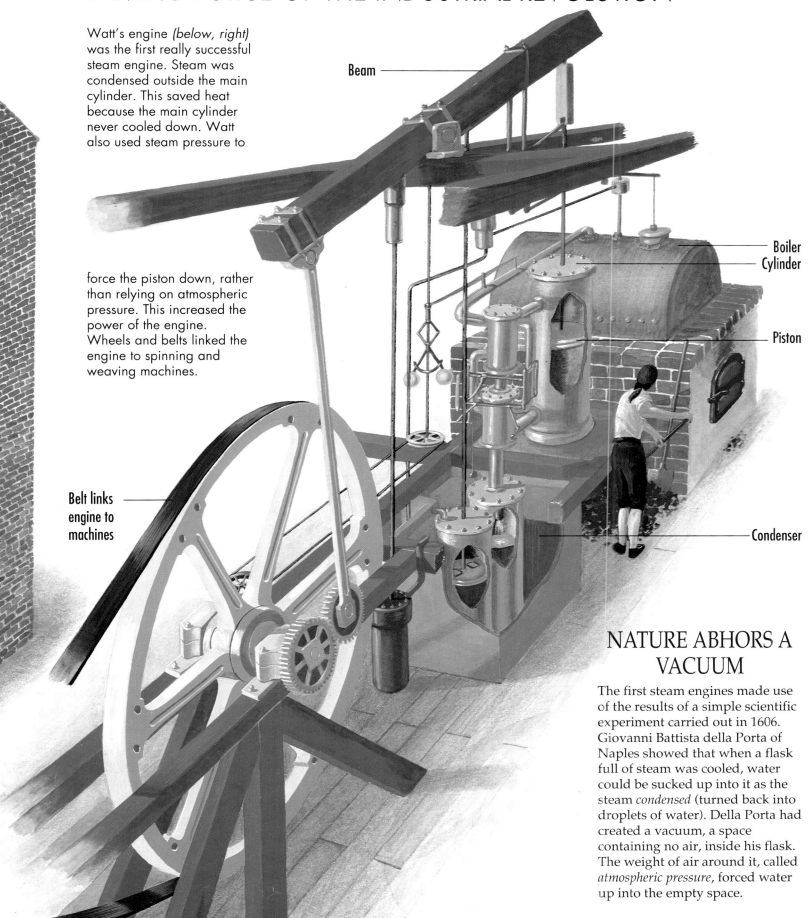

Beam

Boiler

Cylinder

Piston

Belt links engine to machines

Condenser

NATURE ABHORS A VACUUM

The first steam engines made use of the results of a simple scientific experiment carried out in 1606. Giovanni Battista della Porta of Naples showed that when a flask full of steam was cooled, water could be sucked up into it as the steam *condensed* (turned back into droplets of water). Della Porta had created a vacuum, a space containing no air, inside his flask. The weight of air around it, called *atmospheric pressure*, forced water up into the empty space.

13

THE LARGEST LOCOMOTIVE
UNION PACIFIC'S 'BIG BOY'

THE LARGEST, HEAVIEST and most powerful railway locomotive that ever pulled a train was the 'Big Boy'. Between 1941 and 1945, 25 of these giants were built by the American Locomotive Company of Schenectady, New York for the Union Pacific Railroad. They were 40 metres long (about one-and-a-half times the length of a basketball court) and weighed more than 600 tonnes. Each locomotive was able to haul a load six times its own weight up a steep gradient in the mountains of the western United States.

Big Boys had two sets of eight driving wheels. The front set were specially designed to swivel to enable the giant locomotive to go around bends on the twisting mountain railway. No fireman could shovel coal fast enough to keep the furnace stoked up, so a mechanical stoker was used. This machine could deliver 22 tonnes of coal an hour to the firebox. The Big Boys used up a lot of water, too. At top speed they guzzled 50 tonnes of water an hour – about a saucepanful every second!

The illustrations are approximately to scale

The Big Boy locomotives hauled ore trains with more than 70 wagons between Wyoming and Utah, across the Wasatch Mountains.

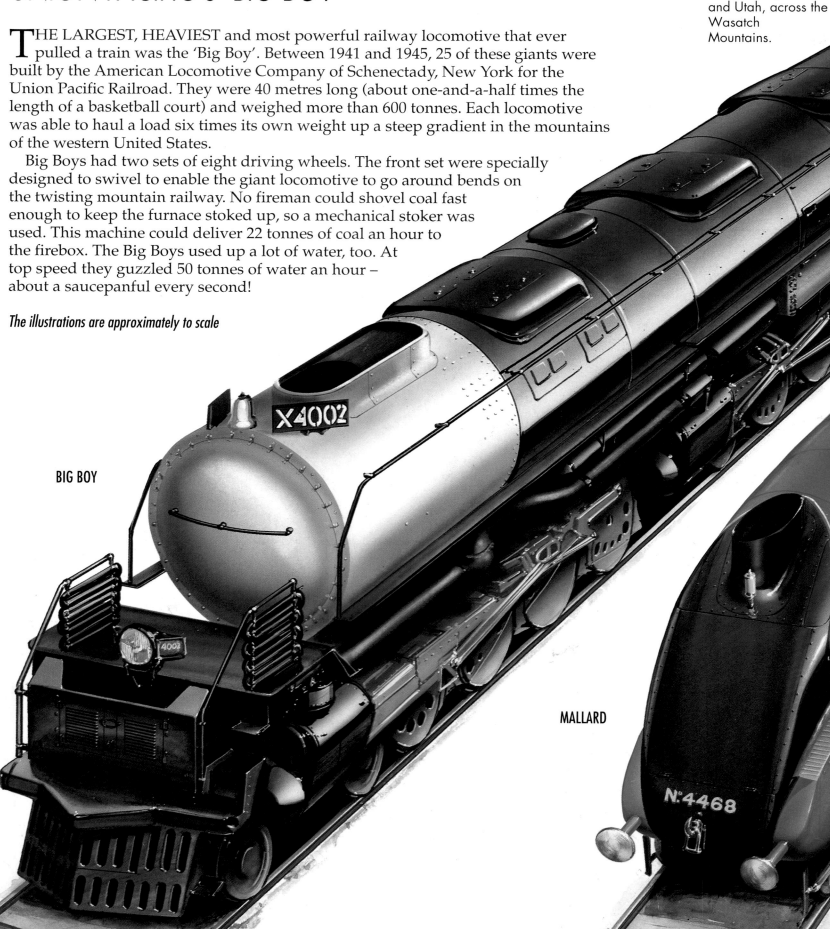

BIG BOY

X4002

MALLARD

No 4468

THE FASTEST STEAM LOCOMOTIVE

A new world record speed for a steam locomotive was set on 3 July 1938. The *Mallard*, a new engine fitted with a streamlined casing, was chosen for the honour. Pulling a seven-coach train between Grantham and Peterborough, England, *Mallard* was timed at a speed of 201.16 km/h over a distance of about 400 m. It was damaged during the run, but was repaired and placed in the Railway Museum, York, England. Its record has stood to this day.

TREVITHICK'S LOCOMOTIVE

THE FIRST TRAINS

The first steam locomotive to run on rails was built by Cornish engineer Richard Trevithick. His four-wheel locomotive made a demonstration run on 22 February 1804, reaching 20 km/h when empty and 8 km/h (a brisk walking-pace) when loaded. Unfortunately, the weight of the train broke the rails! By 1812, stronger tracks had been built between Middleton Colliery and Leeds, England. They carried the first successful steam locomotives.

In 1829, while the new Liverpool and Manchester Railway was being built in northern England, a competition was held to find the best locomotive to run along it. The £500 prize was won easily by the *Rocket*, entered by George and Robert Stephenson. It reached the then breathtaking speed of 46.7 km/h, a world record. For the first time, people would be able to travel on land faster than by horse.

This illustration *(below)* shows the inside of a steam locomotive. Water is heated by the fire tubes in the boiler. The steam is forced into a cylinder where it pushes a piston linked to the driving wheels. When the piston reaches the end of the cylinder, steam is let into the other side, pushing the piston back again.

ROCKET

Boiler   Steam   Piston

Fire-box   Driving wheels   Cylinder

THE FASTEST TRAIN
FRANCE'S ROCKET ON RAILS

THE FRENCH HIGH-SPEED TRAIN, the *Train à Grande Vitesse* or TGV, holds the world speed record for a train travelling on rails. During a test run without passengers between Paris and Tours in 1990, the TGV reached a speed of 515 km/h – half as fast again as a Formula 1 racing car *(see page 44)*. Even in regular service, the TGV easily outpaces any other train. The 425-kilometre journey from Paris to Lyon takes about 2 hours.

The TGV is powered by electric current from an overhead cable. The two locomotives, one at either end of the train, together with its eight passenger cars, are all carefully streamlined, so the train uses up no more fuel than an ordinary train.

Back in the age of steam, if you found yourself in the driver's cab, you would be faced by an array of dials and levers, you would feel the searing heat from the fire-box,

and your ears would be deafened by the pounding noise. The TGV driver's cab is more like a modern office, the noise of the speeding locomotive barely rising above the level of whirring computers. Computers effectively drive the train. The driver checks the train's progress on a computer screen and gives instructions by using a keyboard. A radio links on-board computers with the signalling centre and other trains on the track. Computers also operate the brakes, air-conditioning and other equipment.

The high-speed TGV can travel up slopes four times as steep as most other trains. So the new tracks built for it could be much straighter, saving much of the cost of constructing a level track across hilly country.

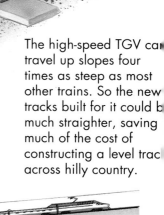

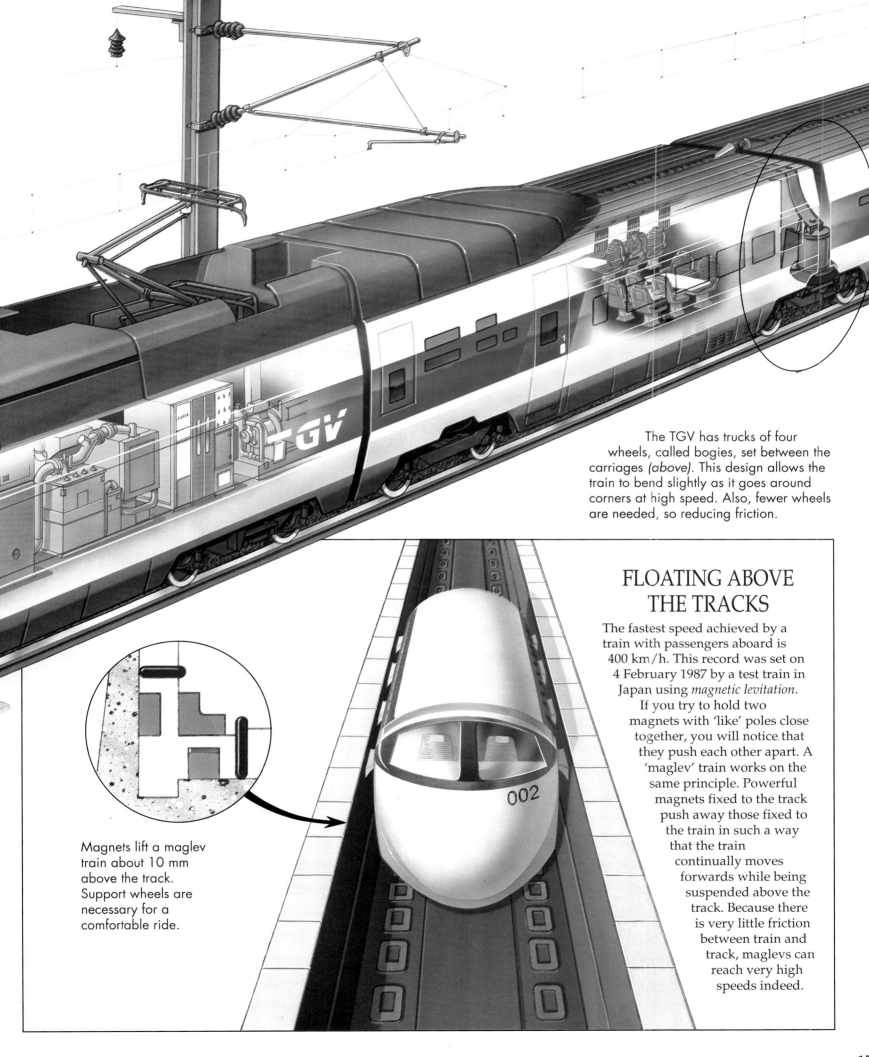

The TGV has trucks of four wheels, called bogies, set between the carriages *(above)*. This design allows the train to bend slightly as it goes around corners at high speed. Also, fewer wheels are needed, so reducing friction.

FLOATING ABOVE THE TRACKS

The fastest speed achieved by a train with passengers aboard is 400 km/h. This record was set on 4 February 1987 by a test train in Japan using *magnetic levitation*. If you try to hold two magnets with 'like' poles close together, you will notice that they push each other apart. A 'maglev' train works on the same principle. Powerful magnets fixed to the track push away those fixed to the train in such a way that the train continually moves forwards while being suspended above the track. Because there is very little friction between train and track, maglevs can reach very high speeds indeed.

Magnets lift a maglev train about 10 mm above the track. Support wheels are necessary for a comfortable ride.

RACING YACHT

The Soviet Typhoon class submarines (above) are the largest ever built. They can stay underwater for years at a time. They were designed to carry missiles that could strike targets almost 9000 km away – just over the distance from London to Los Angeles.

The largest ocean liner of all time was the *Queen Elizabeth* (above). Launched during World War II, she began service as a troop ship. After the war, she plied the oceans as a cruiser until 1968.

BLUE WHALE

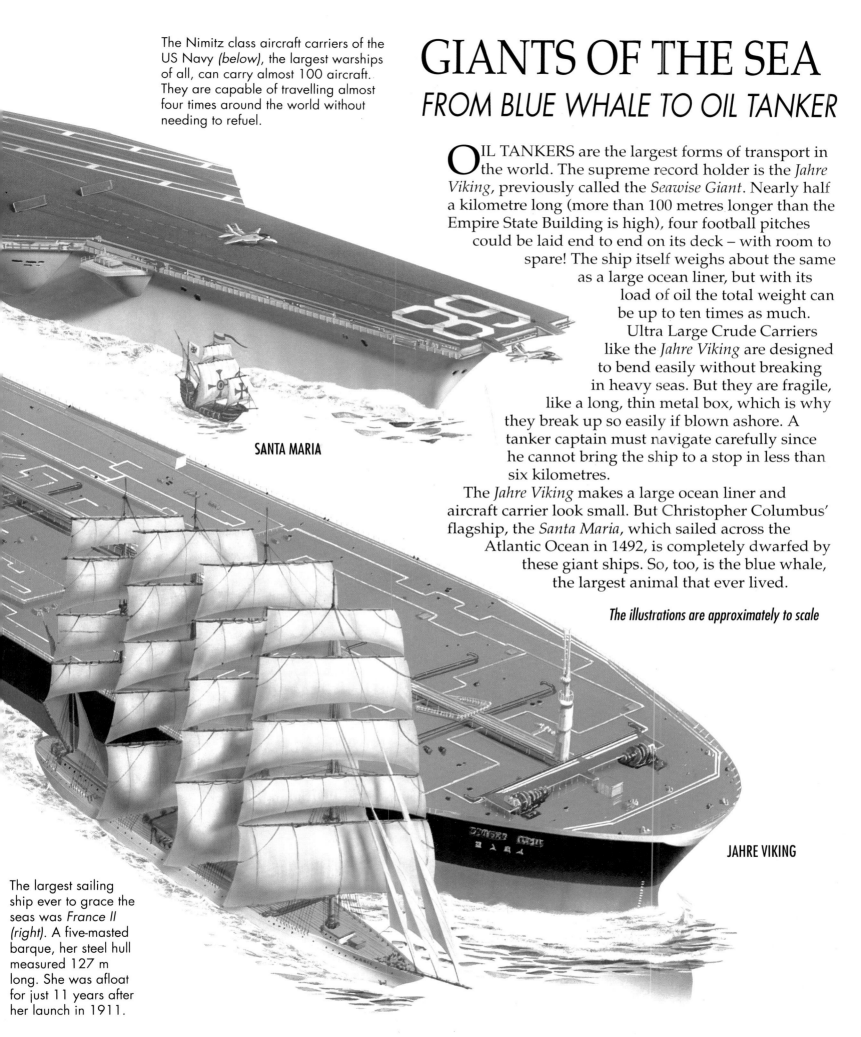

The Nimitz class aircraft carriers of the US Navy *(below)*, the largest warships of all, can carry almost 100 aircraft. They are capable of travelling almost four times around the world without needing to refuel.

GIANTS OF THE SEA
FROM BLUE WHALE TO OIL TANKER

OIL TANKERS are the largest forms of transport in the world. The supreme record holder is the *Jahre Viking*, previously called the *Seawise Giant*. Nearly half a kilometre long (more than 100 metres longer than the Empire State Building is high), four football pitches could be laid end to end on its deck – with room to spare! The ship itself weighs about the same as a large ocean liner, but with its load of oil the total weight can be up to ten times as much.

Ultra Large Crude Carriers like the *Jahre Viking* are designed to bend easily without breaking in heavy seas. But they are fragile, like a long, thin metal box, which is why they break up so easily if blown ashore. A tanker captain must navigate carefully since he cannot bring the ship to a stop in less than six kilometres.

The *Jahre Viking* makes a large ocean liner and aircraft carrier look small. But Christopher Columbus' flagship, the *Santa Maria*, which sailed across the Atlantic Ocean in 1492, is completely dwarfed by these giant ships. So, too, is the blue whale, the largest animal that ever lived.

The illustrations are approximately to scale

SANTA MARIA

JAHRE VIKING

The largest sailing ship ever to grace the seas was *France II (right)*. A five-masted barque, her steel hull measured 127 m long. She was afloat for just 11 years after her launch in 1911.

HUMAN-POWERED VEHICLES
FROM RUNNING MACHINE TO FLYING MACHINE

PEOPLE FLED IN TERROR and horses bolted when Baron von Drais first rode his 'running machine' in 1817. The German inventor sat astride his *draisienne*, which consisted of two wheels, one behind the other, connected by a wooden frame, and moved forwards simply by pushing on the ground with his feet. On good roads, this machine was faster than a horse. It was the fastest land vehicle of its time.

The *draisienne* was the first of a long line of human-powered vehicles, eventually leading to the first human-powered aircraft. In 1839 a Scottish blacksmith, Kirkpatrick Macmillan, built the first real bicycle – one which could be driven without the rider's feet touching the ground – with pedals which turned the back wheel. He was fined five shillings by Glasgow

magistrates when he knocked over a child during a ride around the city streets.

The first really successful pedal-powered bicycle was made in Paris in 1861 by a coach repairer, Pierre Michaux and his son, Ernest. They fitted two pedals to the front wheel of a *draisienne*. The new machine, known as a 'boneshaker', became popular. English inventor James Starley designed a famous version of it in 1870 which became known as the Penny Farthing, after its enormous front wheel (1.5 metres across) and much smaller rear wheel.

Starley later built the Rover safety bicycle. With its strong diamond-shaped frame, equal-sized wheels and geared chain drive, this 1885 machine was the forerunner of all modern bicycles.

Macmillan's bicycle *(left)* had pedals connected with rods to the back wheel. Ernest Michaux's first 'boneshaker' *(centre)* had wood or iron wheels that, as the name suggests, made riding uncomfortable. John Boyd Dunlop, a Belfast vet, introduced air-filled tyres in 1888. The Starley Rover bicycle *(right)* had a chain connecting the pedals to the back wheel.

PEDALLING THROUGH THE AIR

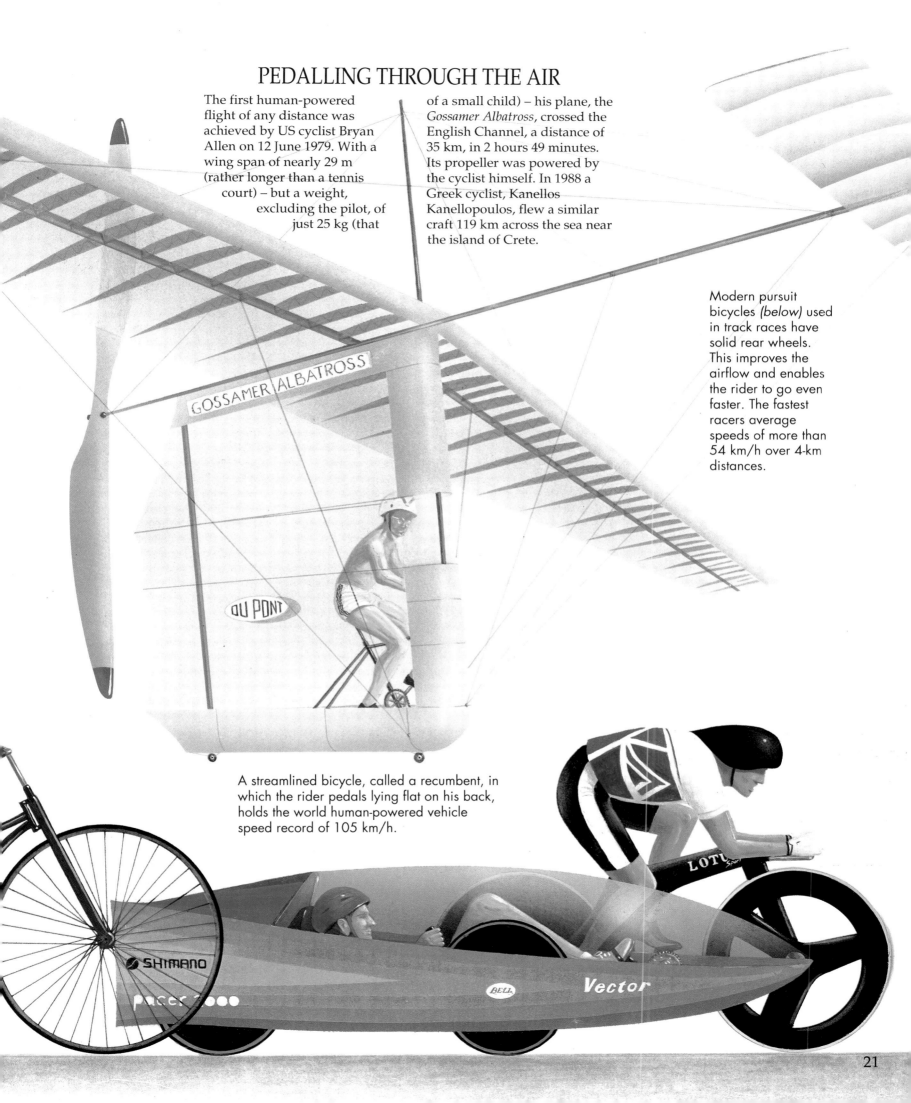

The first human-powered flight of any distance was achieved by US cyclist Bryan Allen on 12 June 1979. With a wing span of nearly 29 m (rather longer than a tennis court) – but a weight, excluding the pilot, of just 25 kg (that of a small child) – his plane, the *Gossamer Albatross*, crossed the English Channel, a distance of 35 km, in 2 hours 49 minutes. Its propeller was powered by the cyclist himself. In 1988 a Greek cyclist, Kanellos Kanellopoulos, flew a similar craft 119 km across the sea near the island of Crete.

Modern pursuit bicycles *(below)* used in track races have solid rear wheels. This improves the airflow and enables the rider to go even faster. The fastest racers average speeds of more than 54 km/h over 4-km distances.

A streamlined bicycle, called a recumbent, in which the rider pedals lying flat on his back, holds the world human-powered vehicle speed record of 105 km/h.

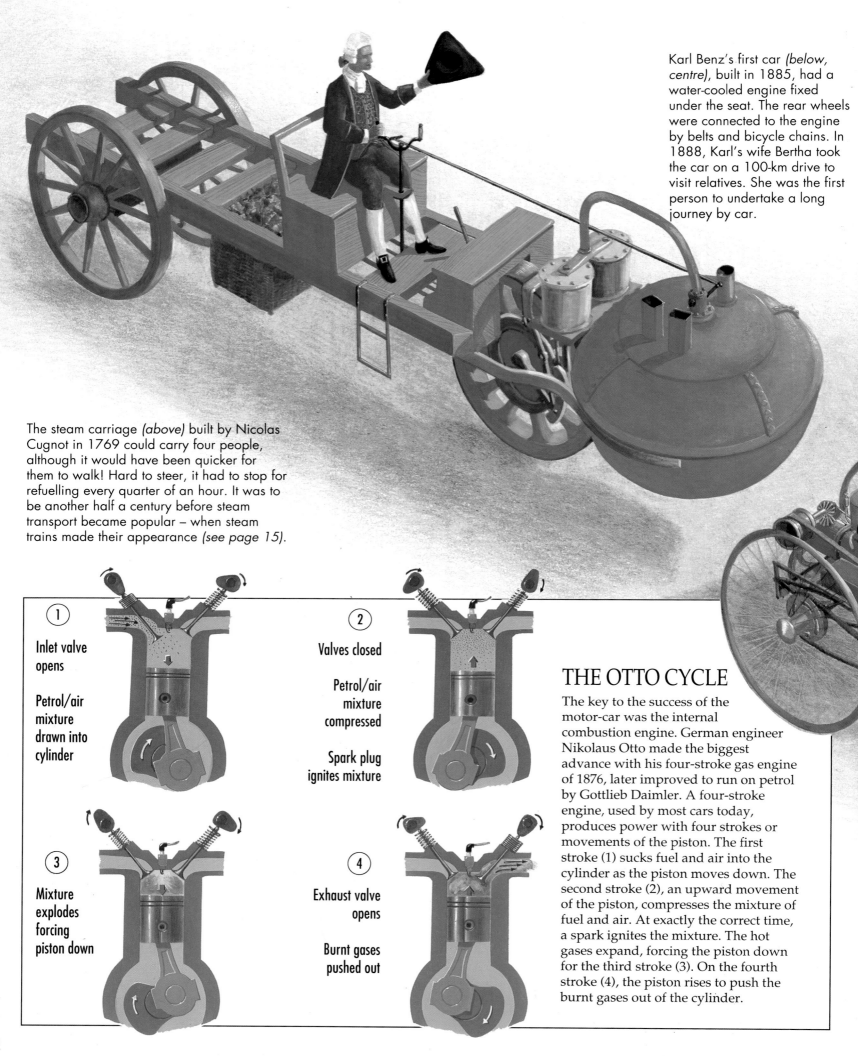

Karl Benz's first car *(below, centre)*, built in 1885, had a water-cooled engine fixed under the seat. The rear wheels were connected to the engine by belts and bicycle chains. In 1888, Karl's wife Bertha took the car on a 100-km drive to visit relatives. She was the first person to undertake a long journey by car.

The steam carriage *(above)* built by Nicolas Cugnot in 1769 could carry four people, although it would have been quicker for them to walk! Hard to steer, it had to stop for refuelling every quarter of an hour. It was to be another half a century before steam transport became popular – when steam trains made their appearance *(see page 15)*.

① Inlet valve opens

Petrol/air mixture drawn into cylinder

② Valves closed

Petrol/air mixture compressed

Spark plug ignites mixture

③ Mixture explodes forcing piston down

④ Exhaust valve opens

Burnt gases pushed out

THE OTTO CYCLE

The key to the success of the motor-car was the internal combustion engine. German engineer Nikolaus Otto made the biggest advance with his four-stroke gas engine of 1876, later improved to run on petrol by Gottlieb Daimler. A four-stroke engine, used by most cars today, produces power with four strokes or movements of the piston. The first stroke (1) sucks fuel and air into the cylinder as the piston moves down. The second stroke (2), an upward movement of the piston, compresses the mixture of fuel and air. At exactly the correct time, a spark ignites the mixture. The hot gases expand, forcing the piston down for the third stroke (3). On the fourth stroke (4), the piston rises to push the burnt gases out of the cylinder.

In 1885, a few months before Benz produced his motor-car, Gottlieb Daimler attached a petrol engine to a wooden-framed bicycle *(below, right)*. His 17-year-old son Paul rode the world's first motor vehicle about 17 km around the streets of Cannstatt, Germany. During the trip, the saddle, fitted to close to the top of the engine, burst into flames!

THE FIRST CARS
ENTER THE HORSELESS CARRIAGE

THE FIRST SELF-PROPELLED land vehicles were powered by steam engines *(see page 12)*. Frenchman Nicolas Cugnot built the first steam carriage in 1769. Designed to pull heavy guns, it caused the world's first motor accident when it crashed into a wall at its top speed of 5 km/h!

The age of the automobile really began in 1885 when German engineer Karl Benz successfully fitted a petrol engine to a three-wheeled tricycle. To begin with, his new car lurched and spluttered dangerously around the streets of Mannheim, but a smooth ride was soon achieved. The local newspaper reported: "Without the aid of any human element, the vehicle rolled onwards, taking bends in its stride and avoiding all oncoming traffic and pedestrians. It was followed by a crowd of running and breathless youngsters."

Meanwhile, another German engineer, Gottlieb Daimler was hard at work. He had already invented a petrol-driven motorcycle and was, in 1886, to build the first four-wheeled car, a 'horseless carriage' fitted with a powerful petrol engine.

In 1890, two French machine toolmakers, René Panhard and Emile Levassor, began making cars using Daimler engines. The following year they produced a model *(right)* that can be described as the first modern car. Fitted beneath a square bonnet at the front, its engine was connected to the rear wheels by a clutch and gears. Other modern devices made their first appearances in early French designs: hollow rubber tyres were first used on a 1895 Peugeot and a propeller shaft replaced chain drive in the first Renault built in 1898.

GOING FOR THE LAND SPEED RECORD

FROM EARLY ELECTRICS TO MODERN JETS

THE FIRST WORLD LAND SPEED RECORD was set at Achères near Paris in 1898, just 13 years after the motor car had been first invented. Count Gaston de Chasseloup-Laubat drove an electric car, the *Jeantaud*, at a speed of 63.14 km/h. Medical experts at the time declared it would be impossible to breathe at these speeds, and that the driver's heart would surely stop!

Chasseloup-Laubat improved on his own record a year later, taking it up to 93.7 km/h. In the same year, Camille Jenatzy became the first motorist to exceed 100 km/h. His bullet-shaped electric car, called *La Jamais Contente* ('never-satisfied') held the record for three years. A spectator described the car as moving "with a subdued noise like the rustling of wings, scarcely seeming to touch the ground".

Steam-powered cars were among the early land speed record holders. One reached a speed of 120 km/h in 1902 but they were soon to give way to faster petrol-engined cars. The *Mors*, the first of the breed, broke the record in 1902. In 1927, the 300 km/h barrier was breached by the first car specially built for the record attempt, the *Sunbeam*. This streamlined vehicle, driven by Englishman Henry Segrave, was powered by two aircraft engines. The record was then pushed steadily higher by a series of cars with more and more powerful engines. The largest of these, the *Thunderbolt*, reached 555 km/h in 1939.

In 1964, however, the petrol engine faced a new type of competition. Jet and rocket-powered cars were allowed to enter the speed contest for the first time. A jet-engined car, the *Spirit of America*, soon took the record to over 800 km/h in that year. The first rocket-powered car, *Blue Flame*, driven by American Gary Gabelich shot past 1000 km/h in 1970.

The land speed racers of the early 1900s were the fastest vehicles on Earth, faster even than the primitive aircraft that were taking to the skies at the time. Racing at speeds we would consider even today extremely fast (more than 150 km/h) on bumpy road surfaces, many of the drivers risked their lives.

JEANTAUD
March 1899
93.7 km/h
First electric-powered record holder

SERPOLLET
April 1902 120.8 km/h
First steam-powered record holder

GOBRON-BRILLIÉ
July 1904
166.6 km/h
First record holder over 100 mph

LA JAMAIS CONTENTE
December 1899
105.9 km/h
First record holder over 100 km/h

MORS
November 1902
124.1 km/h
First petrol-powered record holder

BLITZEN BENZ
November 1909
202.7 km/h
First record holder over 200 km/h

BLUEBIRD
February 1932
408.9 km/h
First record holder over 400 km/h

SUNBEAM
March 1927
328 km/h
First record holder over 300 km/h and 200 mph

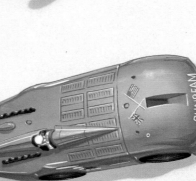

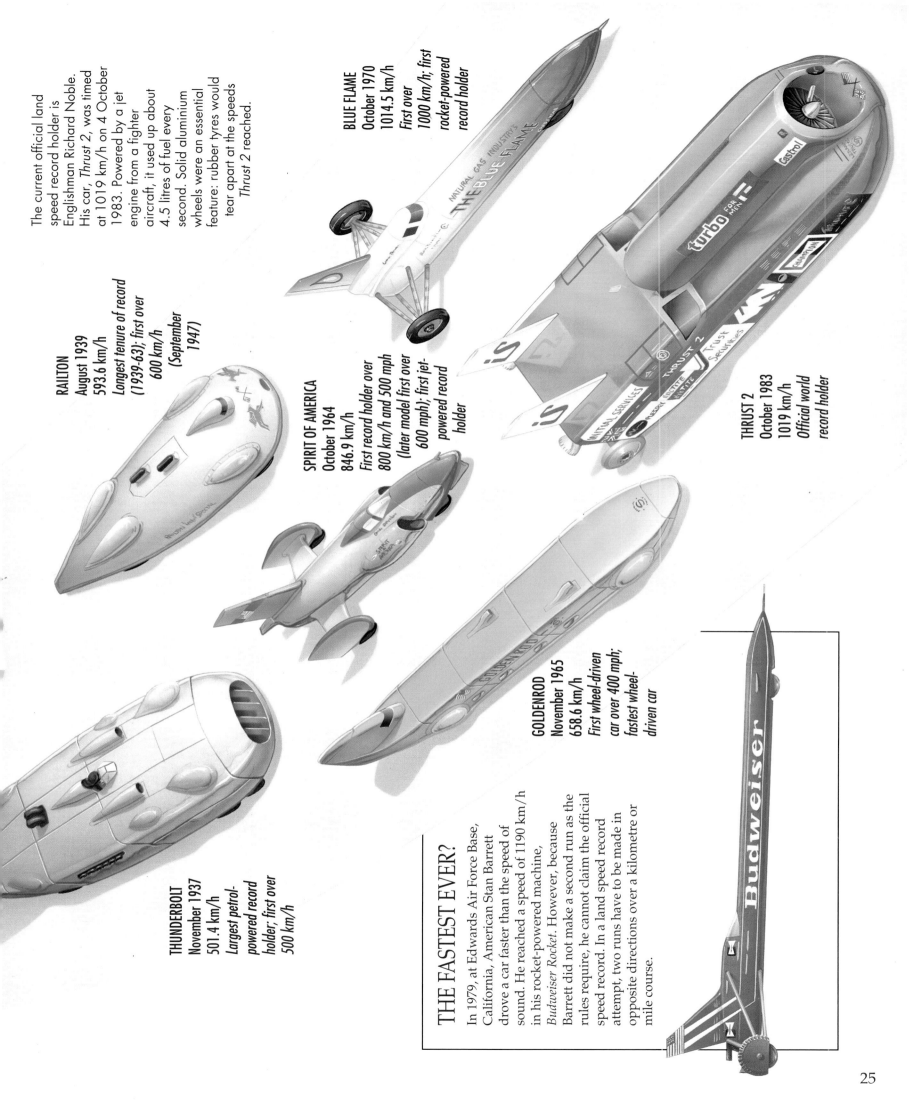

The current official land speed record holder is Englishman Richard Noble. His car, *Thrust 2*, was timed at 1019 km/h on 4 October 1983. Powered by a jet engine from a fighter aircraft, it used up about 4.5 litres of fuel every second. Solid aluminium wheels were an essential feature: rubber tyres would tear apart at the speeds *Thrust 2* reached.

BLUE FLAME
October 1970
1014.5 km/h
First over 1000 km/h; first rocket-powered record holder

RAILTON
August 1939
593.6 km/h
Longest tenure of record (1939-63); first over 600 km/h (September 1947)

SPIRIT OF AMERICA
October 1964
846.9 km/h
First record holder over 800 km/h and 500 mph (later model first over 600 mph); first jet-powered record holder

THRUST 2
October 1983
1019 km/h
Official world record holder

THUNDERBOLT
November 1937
501.4 km/h
Largest petrol-powered record holder; first over 500 km/h

GOLDENROD
November 1965
658.6 km/h
First wheel-driven car over 400 mph; fastest wheel-driven car

THE FASTEST EVER?

In 1979, at Edwards Air Force Base, California, American Stan Barrett drove a car faster than the speed of sound. He reached a speed of 1190 km/h in his rocket-powered machine, *Budweiser Rocket*. However, because Barrett did not make a second run as the rules require, he cannot claim the official speed record. In a land speed record attempt, two runs have to be made in opposite directions over a kilometre or mile course.

25

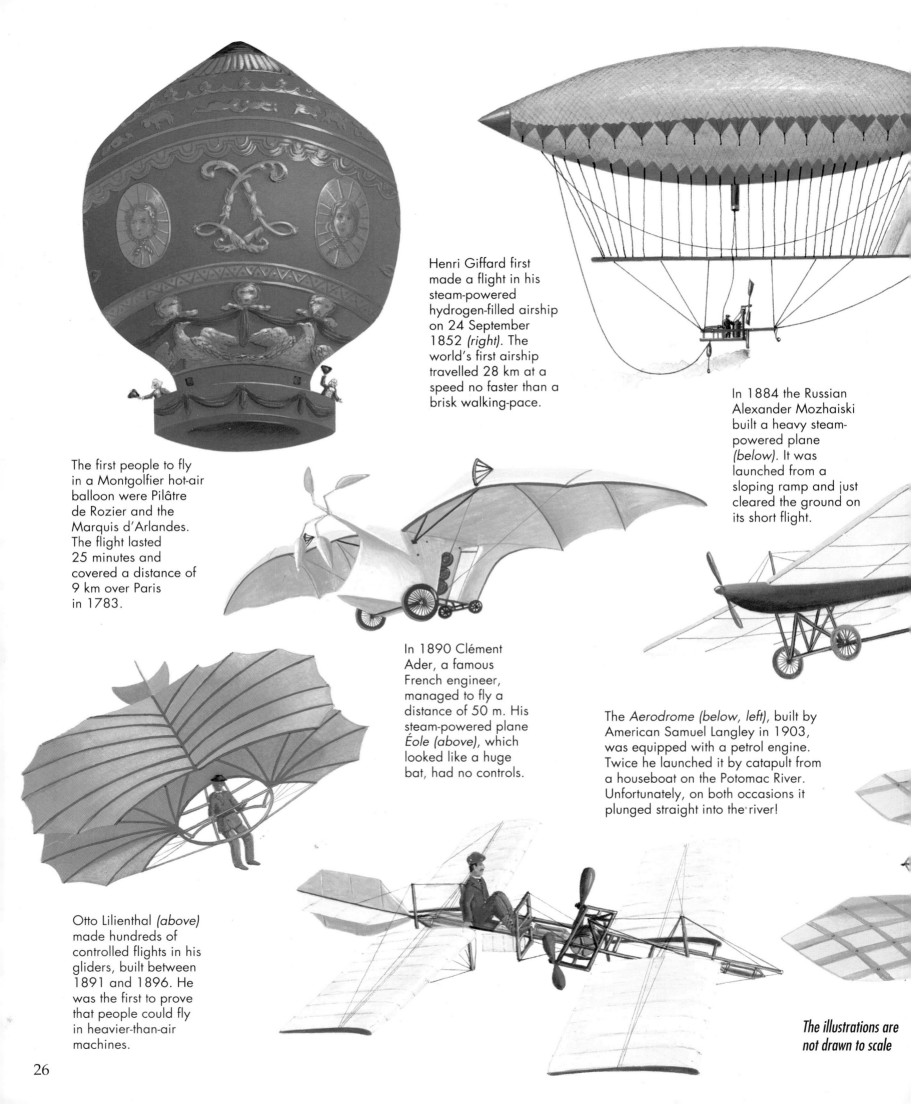

Henri Giffard first made a flight in his steam-powered hydrogen-filled airship on 24 September 1852 *(right)*. The world's first airship travelled 28 km at a speed no faster than a brisk walking-pace.

The first people to fly in a Montgolfier hot-air balloon were Pilâtre de Rozier and the Marquis d'Arlandes. The flight lasted 25 minutes and covered a distance of 9 km over Paris in 1783.

In 1884 the Russian Alexander Mozhaiski built a heavy steam-powered plane *(below)*. It was launched from a sloping ramp and just cleared the ground on its short flight.

In 1890 Clément Ader, a famous French engineer, managed to fly a distance of 50 m. His steam-powered plane *Éole (above)*, which looked like a huge bat, had no controls.

The *Aerodrome (below, left)*, built by American Samuel Langley in 1903, was equipped with a petrol engine. Twice he launched it by catapult from a houseboat on the Potomac River. Unfortunately, on both occasions it plunged straight into the river!

Otto Lilienthal *(above)* made hundreds of controlled flights in his gliders, built between 1891 and 1896. He was the first to prove that people could fly in heavier-than-air machines.

The illustrations are not drawn to scale

THE FIRST AIRCRAFT
THE QUEST FOR FLIGHT

In 1849 a glider built by George Cayley *(right)* was launched from a hillside with a 10 year-old boy on board. It managed to travel about 500 metres.

Félix du Temple built the first powered aeroplane, a small model with a clockwork engine, in 1857. A full-sized steam-powered plane *(right)* took off from a steep ramp 17 years later. This was the first-known hop by a manned, powered aeroplane.

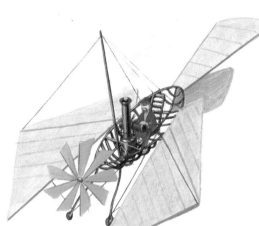

THE FIRST SUCCESSFUL flying machines were balloons filled with hot air. A hot-air balloon was sent up on 15 June 1783 by two French brothers, Joseph and Etienne Montgolfier. It rose to a height of about 1800 metres. Later that year they demonstrated their invention to the King and Queen of France. This time, the balloon carried three passengers – a sheep, a cockerel and a duck. After a short flight, the animals landed safely. On 21 November 1783, the first human passengers, Jean Pilâtre de Rozier and the Marquis d'Arlandes, braved a flight in a Montgolfier balloon. They were the first aviators in history.

It was Englishman George Cayley who designed the modern aeroplane, with wings and a tail like those flying today. However, none of his machines ever flew for long: in the mid-19th century no engine yet invented was light enough to power a piloted flying machine.

The first people to fix a petrol engine to an aeroplane and achieve a controlled flight were the American brothers, Wilbur and Orville Wright. Their aircraft *Flyer I* first flew on 17 December 1903.

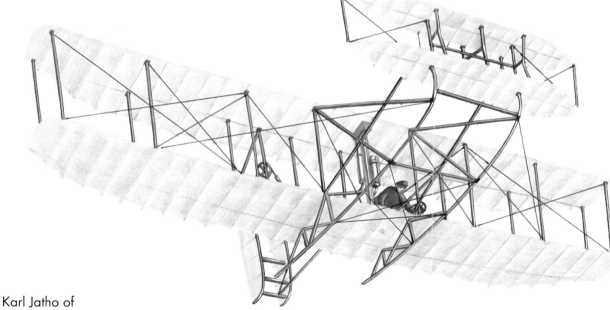

Karl Jatho of Germany came near to claiming the record for the first flight. Although it lacked controls, his kite-like aeroplane *(left)* made a number of flights of up to 60 metres.

FIRST CONTROLLED FLIGHT

The historic first flight of the Wright brothers' *Flyer I (above)* took place on sand dunes near Kitty Hawk, North Carolina. With Orville at the controls, *Flyer* remained aloft for about 12 seconds and flew a distance of just 36 m, less than the wing-span of many modern airliners. By changing the angle of the wing tips (warping), the Wrights could control their aircraft. Theirs was indisputably the first controlled, powered flight.

THE FIRST HELICOPTERS
FROM FLYING TOP TO SIKORSKY

THE WAY IN WHICH a helicopter flies has been understood for many centuries. A flying top, invented by the Chinese around 500 BC, was a small propeller that flew upwards when the stick on which it was balanced was spun rapidly. The propeller 'bit' into the air, producing uplift. This method of flight worked well for small toys but how could a full-sized machine capable of carrying people through the air be built? Only when light petrol engines (*see page 22*) came available in the early 1900s would the helicopter at last take to the skies.

The first take-off by a manned helicopter was achieved in 1907 by Frenchman Paul Cornu. However, he and other early helicopter pilots were not yet able to control their machines. They tended to twist in the opposite direction to the blades when the helicopter moved forwards. The German aircraft designer Heinrich Focke and Russian-born American engineer Igor Sikorsky both came up with the answers. Fitting two rotors, each turning in opposite directions, solved the problem.

A FLYING TOP

Leonardo da Vinci, Italian painter, scientist and engineer was fascinated with the idea of helicopter flight. His design, produced around 1500, had a corkscrew-shaped rotor which, he thought, would soar upwards through the air as it spun. To power the machine, the pilot simply pulled sharply on a rope wound around the central column – just as with a Chinese flying top. Not surprisingly, his machine never flew! Leonardo was, however, the first to use the word 'helicopter', which he derived from the Greek for 'spiral wing'.

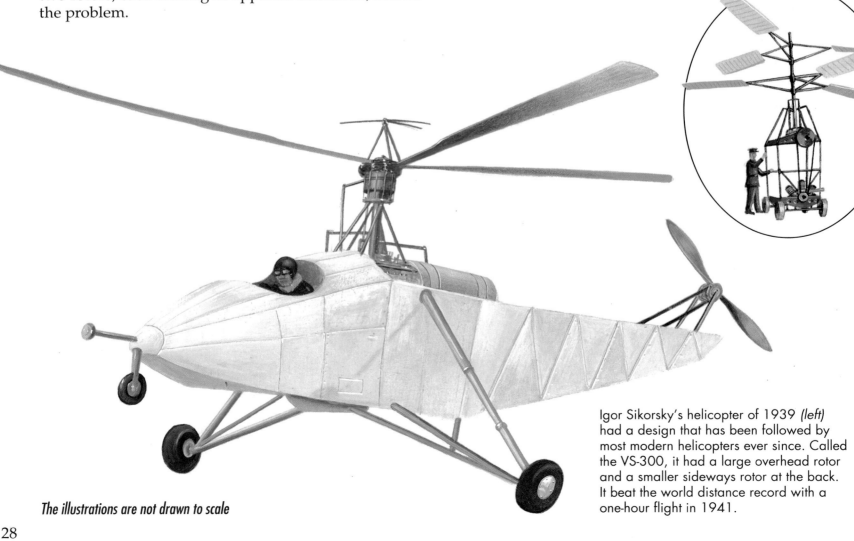

The illustrations are not drawn to scale

Igor Sikorsky's helicopter of 1939 *(left)* had a design that has been followed by most modern helicopters ever since. Called the VS-300, it had a large overhead rotor and a smaller sideways rotor at the back. It beat the world distance record with a one-hour flight in 1941.

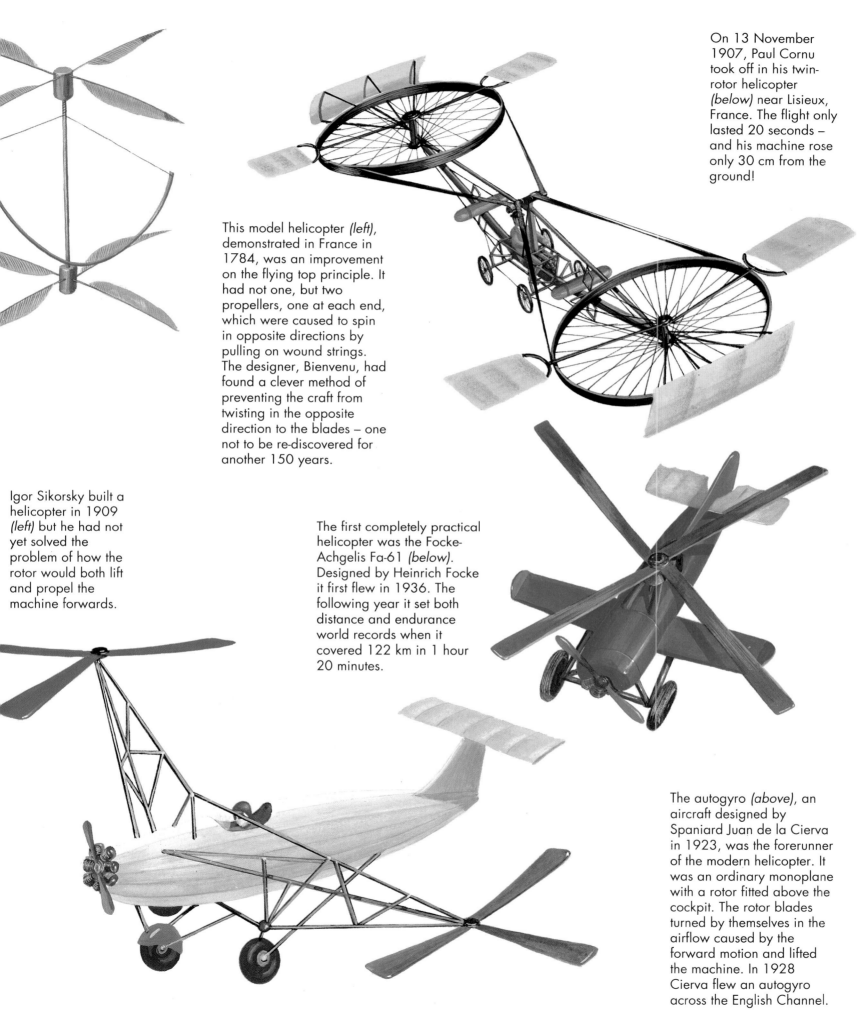

On 13 November 1907, Paul Cornu took off in his twin-rotor helicopter *(below)* near Lisieux, France. The flight only lasted 20 seconds – and his machine rose only 30 cm from the ground!

This model helicopter *(left)*, demonstrated in France in 1784, was an improvement on the flying top principle. It had not one, but two propellers, one at each end, which were caused to spin in opposite directions by pulling on wound strings. The designer, Bienvenu, had found a clever method of preventing the craft from twisting in the opposite direction to the blades – one not to be re-discovered for another 150 years.

Igor Sikorsky built a helicopter in 1909 *(left)* but he had not yet solved the problem of how the rotor would both lift and propel the machine forwards.

The first completely practical helicopter was the Focke-Achgelis Fa-61 *(below)*. Designed by Heinrich Focke it first flew in 1936. The following year it set both distance and endurance world records when it covered 122 km in 1 hour 20 minutes.

The autogyro *(above)*, an aircraft designed by Spaniard Juan de la Cierva in 1923, was the forerunner of the modern helicopter. It was an ordinary monoplane with a rotor fitted above the cockpit. The rotor blades turned by themselves in the airflow caused by the forward motion and lifted the machine. In 1928 Cierva flew an autogyro across the English Channel.

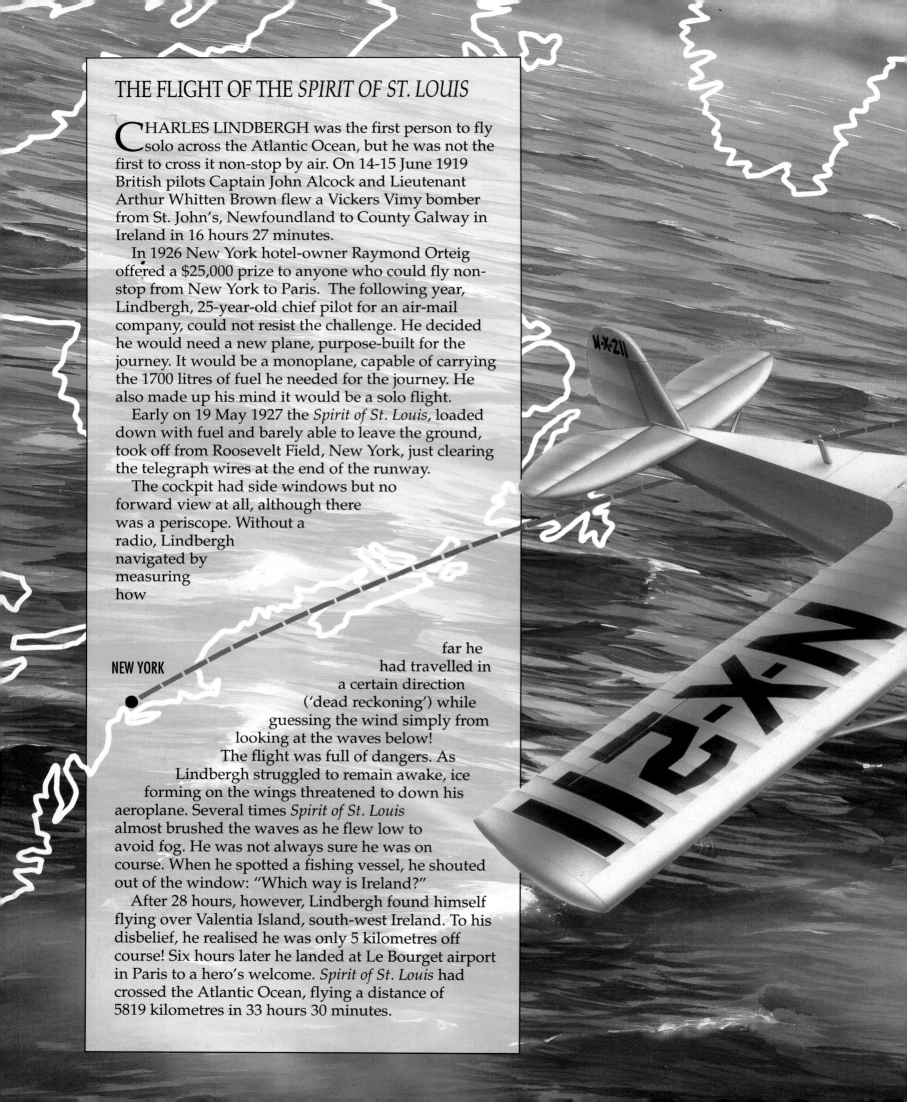

THE FLIGHT OF THE *SPIRIT OF ST. LOUIS*

CHARLES LINDBERGH was the first person to fly solo across the Atlantic Ocean, but he was not the first to cross it non-stop by air. On 14-15 June 1919 British pilots Captain John Alcock and Lieutenant Arthur Whitten Brown flew a Vickers Vimy bomber from St. John's, Newfoundland to County Galway in Ireland in 16 hours 27 minutes.

In 1926 New York hotel-owner Raymond Orteig offered a $25,000 prize to anyone who could fly non-stop from New York to Paris. The following year, Lindbergh, 25-year-old chief pilot for an air-mail company, could not resist the challenge. He decided he would need a new plane, purpose-built for the journey. It would be a monoplane, capable of carrying the 1700 litres of fuel he needed for the journey. He also made up his mind it would be a solo flight.

Early on 19 May 1927 the *Spirit of St. Louis*, loaded down with fuel and barely able to leave the ground, took off from Roosevelt Field, New York, just clearing the telegraph wires at the end of the runway.

The cockpit had side windows but no forward view at all, although there was a periscope. Without a radio, Lindbergh navigated by measuring how

NEW YORK

far he had travelled in a certain direction ('dead reckoning') while guessing the wind simply from looking at the waves below!

The flight was full of dangers. As Lindbergh struggled to remain awake, ice forming on the wings threatened to down his aeroplane. Several times *Spirit of St. Louis* almost brushed the waves as he flew low to avoid fog. He was not always sure he was on course. When he spotted a fishing vessel, he shouted out of the window: "Which way is Ireland?"

After 28 hours, however, Lindbergh found himself flying over Valentia Island, south-west Ireland. To his disbelief, he realised he was only 5 kilometres off course! Six hours later he landed at Le Bourget airport in Paris to a hero's welcome. *Spirit of St. Louis* had crossed the Atlantic Ocean, flying a distance of 5819 kilometres in 33 hours 30 minutes.

FIRST SOLO TRANSATLANTIC FLIGHT
LINDBERGH'S FAMOUS JOURNEY

PARIS

Spirit of St. Louis

THE FASTEST JET AIRCRAFT
LOCKHEED SR-71 BLACKBIRD

THE FASTEST JET AIRCRAFT ever to have flown was an American spyplane, the Lockheed SR-71. Known as 'Blackbird' because of its sleek, black appearance, it was designed to fly fast and high over enemy territory photographing military bases on the ground. From a height of almost 25 kilometres Blackbird's powerful cameras could take a clear shot of a car number plate!

Blackbird's top speed was 3911 km/h – about three times the speed of sound. Its two engines produced more power than those of a large ocean liner. On 1 September 1974 it really showed what it could do. That day it made the fastest ever flight across the Atlantic Ocean, crossing from New York to London in just under 1 hour 55 minutes (a normal flight in an airliner takes around seven hours).

The Lockheed SR-71 was taken out of service in 1990. Some military experts think that the US Air Force may be developing an even faster jet. Called Aurora, it may be capable of flying nearly 30 kilometres high at twice Blackbird's speed!

The illustrations are approximately to scale

The first aircraft to fly faster than sound was a rocket-powered aeroplane called *Glamorous Glennis*. On 14 October 1947 Chuck Yeager of the US Air Force flew the X-1, as it was officially known, at a speed of 1126 km/h above the Mojave Desert in California.

JET ENGINE

ROCKET ENGINE

FASTEST OF ALL

On 3 October 1967 US pilot William Knight flew a rocket-powered plane at a speed of 7274 km/h – nearly seven times the speed of sound. This aircraft, the X-15 (left), could not take off from the ground and was carried aloft underneath a large transporter plane. When the transporter reached its maximum altitude, the X-15's rocket engines ignited and it blasted away to the record. Like Blackbird, the X-15 was built to withstand high temperatures generated at high speeds: its outer skin became 14 times hotter than boiling water during flight.

The X-15 holds more than one record. Unlike jet engines, its rocket-powered engines did not need air to enable them to work. So the X-15 could fly much higher than jet aircraft, to levels of the atmosphere where the air is very thin indeed (see page 40). On 22 August 1963 the X-15 reached a height of 107,960 m, a record altitude for any aircraft.

As thin as an aluminium can, Blackbird's metal skin was painted with a special heat-radiating black paint that could withstand temperatures of over 300° C – the sort of temperatures it experienced travelling at high speeds. As it sped along, it grew nearly 80 cm in length as the metal expanded.

JETS AND ROCKETS

In a jet engine, air enters a compressor, or fan, at its front end. The fan compresses the air (squeezes it into a smaller space) and feeds it through to the combustion chamber. Here, fuel is sprayed in and the mixture ignited. The hot gas produced expands and blasts out the rear of the engine. The gases streaming backwards push the engine – and the aircraft attached to it – forwards, just as when air is suddenly let out of a balloon, that flies forwards, too.

A rocket can operate in space where there is no air. In a solid fuel rocket (left) the fuel burns rapidly, producing a large amount of hot gas. The gas blasts from the rear of the rocket, driving it forwards, just as with a jet engine.

GIANTS OF THE AIR
TRANSPORTERS, HELICOPTERS, AIRLINERS AND AIRSHIPS

THE BIGGEST FLYING MACHINES ever to take to the skies were the airships built in the 1920s and 1930s. These flying giants were the airliners of their day. They flew across the Atlantic – sometimes all the way around the world – but they were slow: the fastest airship could only reach a speed of 131 km/h. The first airship to cross the Atlantic Ocean was the British R-34: the trip took 90 hours. A modern airliner takes only about 7 hours to make the trip.

The largest aeroplane ever built is the Russian Antonov An-225. First flown in 1988, this giant plane is about 600 times the weight of a car. It was built to transport the Russian version of the space shuttle, known as Buran, to its launching-pad. Buran was not successful, so other tasks have had to be found to make use of its vast cargo compartments. It was pressed into service during the Gulf crisis of 1990-1, carrying refugees from Kuwait to safety.

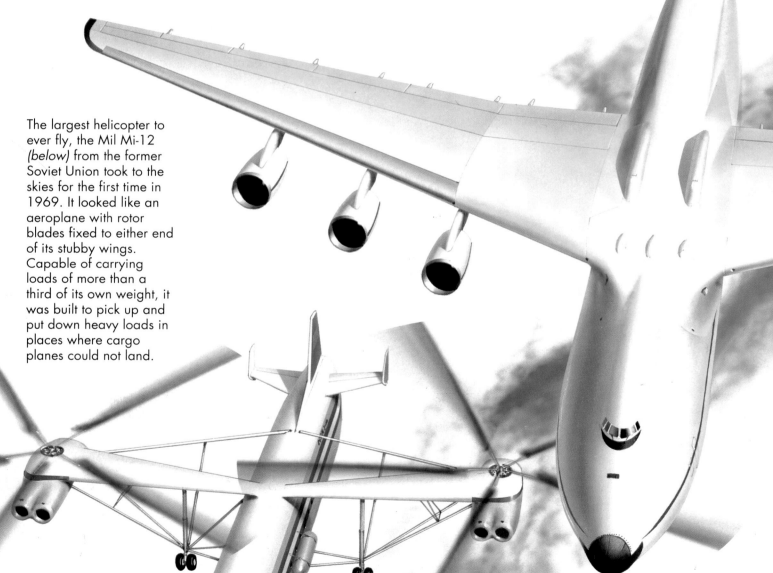

The largest helicopter to ever fly, the Mil Mi-12 *(below)* from the former Soviet Union took to the skies for the first time in 1969. It looked like an aeroplane with rotor blades fixed to either end of its stubby wings. Capable of carrying loads of more than a third of its own weight, it was built to pick up and put down heavy loads in places where cargo planes could not land.

The wingspan of the Antonov An-225 *(above)* is 73 m, nearly twice the distance of the Wright brothers' first flight in *Flyer II*!

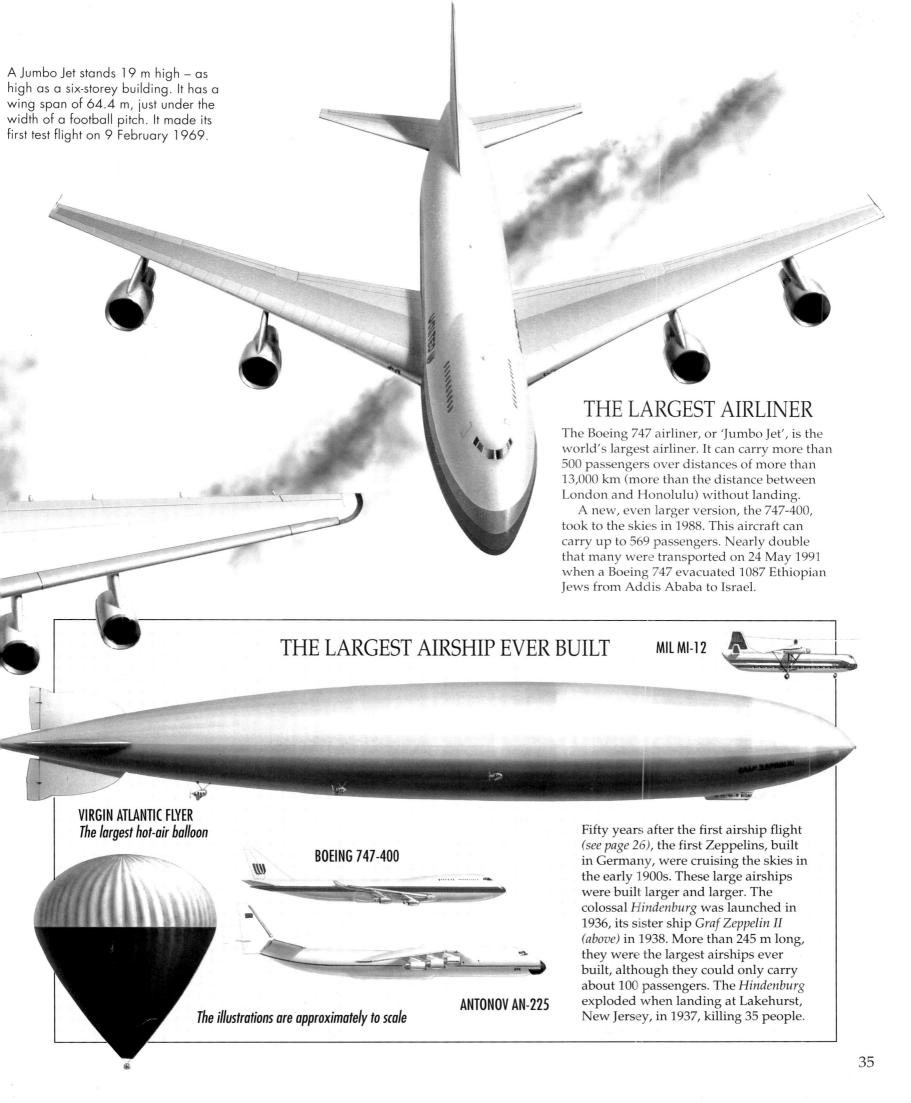

A Jumbo Jet stands 19 m high – as high as a six-storey building. It has a wing span of 64.4 m, just under the width of a football pitch. It made its first test flight on 9 February 1969.

THE LARGEST AIRLINER

The Boeing 747 airliner, or 'Jumbo Jet', is the world's largest airliner. It can carry more than 500 passengers over distances of more than 13,000 km (more than the distance between London and Honolulu) without landing.

A new, even larger version, the 747-400, took to the skies in 1988. This aircraft can carry up to 569 passengers. Nearly double that many were transported on 24 May 1991 when a Boeing 747 evacuated 1087 Ethiopian Jews from Addis Ababa to Israel.

THE LARGEST AIRSHIP EVER BUILT

MIL MI-12

VIRGIN ATLANTIC FLYER
The largest hot-air balloon

BOEING 747-400

ANTONOV AN-225

The illustrations are approximately to scale

Fifty years after the first airship flight *(see page 26)*, the first Zeppelins, built in Germany, were cruising the skies in the early 1900s. These large airships were built larger and larger. The colossal *Hindenburg* was launched in 1936, its sister ship *Graf Zeppelin II* (above) in 1938. More than 245 m long, they were the largest airships ever built, although they could only carry about 100 passengers. The *Hindenburg* exploded when landing at Lakehurst, New Jersey, in 1937, killing 35 people.

35

THE LARGEST ROCKET

AND FAMOUS FIRSTS IN SPACE TECHNOLOGY

TO GET INTO SPACE, a vehicle must overcome the pull of the Earth's gravity. In practice, it must reach a speed of at least 28,500 km/h – or ten times the speed of a rifle bullet. Only immensely powerful rockets (*see page 33*) can achieve such speeds.

The first rockets, built by US inventor Robert Goddard in 1926, were only 1 metre tall. The Vostok rocket which put the first satellite into orbit more than 30 years later was 35 metres high. The Apollo astronauts were carried into space on their way to the Moon in 1969 in a Saturn V. As high as a 30-storey skyscraper, the 111-metre rocket was the largest ever built. The open building used to house Saturn V was so vast that a special air-conditioning system was needed to stop clouds forming and rain falling inside! Saturn V was 50 times as powerful as a Boeing 747 jumbo jet. The most powerful rocket today is the Russian *Energia*. Its four engines are capable of carrying a load as heavy as 24 family cars into orbit. Its original purpose was to launch a space shuttle and perhaps even to send a spaceship to Mars. The former Soviet Union's space programme now faces an uncertain future, however.

The illustrations are approximately to scale

INSIDE SATURN V

Saturn V (*right*), like all launch vehicles, is made from several separate rockets, or stages, joined together. The first rocket is at the bottom and lifts the other stages into the air. When that first rocket runs out of fuel, it drops to the ground. Then the second stage rocket fires. The second stage, too, falls away when its fuel is gone. Then the third stage fires and lifts the spacecraft (in this case, the Apollo Command and Lunar Modules with astronauts on board) into orbit.

PIONEER 10

SPACE PIONEER

In January 1993, the US space probe Pioneer 10 (*right*) was 8.5 billion km from Earth. Even at that distance, its radio signal can still be picked up by powerful receivers. It carries a plaque showing where it came from, should any intelligent life from another solar system come across it! Pioneer 10 is the most distant man-made object, a record that will one day be beaten by another space probe, Voyager 1, which is moving faster.

The US Space Shuttle *Columbia (left)* became the world's first re-usable space-craft when it made its second flight in November 1981.

The Soviet Vostok *(below)* rocket carried the first artificial satellite into orbit. Called Sputnik 1 *(below, left)*, the satellite was launched on 4 October 1957 and remained in orbit for 92 days.

he first-ever rocket
was launched on
6 March 1926, by
JS inventor Robert
Hutchings Goddard
bottom, left). Using
iquid gases for fuel, it
eached a height
f 12.5 m.

he first long-range
quid-fuel rocket was
ne German V2
bottom, right), built in
942. It was 14 m
ong and had a range
f 320 km.

SPUTNIK 1

V2 ROCKET

GODDARD'S ROCKET

FIRST TO THE MOON
THE FLIGHT OF APOLLO 11

THE FIRST LANDING by a manned spacecraft on another body in the Solar System took place on 20 July 1969 when Apollo 11 touched down on the surface of the Moon. A few hours later, US astronaut Neil Armstrong became the first person to step onto the lunar surface.

The spacecraft which took Armstrong and his fellow astronauts Edwin Aldrin and Michael Collins to the Moon was built in several sections, each with a different function. The Command Module (CM), located in the nose of Apollo 11, was both the control centre and cramped living quarters for the crew. The Service Module (SM) contained the main rocket engine used to power the spacecraft. The Lunar Module (LM) was in two parts: both would descend to the Moon itself, but only the upper section would lift off again.

Five more manned landings followed, the last in 1972. The Moon rocks collected were the most expensive rocks in history. The Apollo astronauts collected 380 kilograms of rocks and soil from six different locations. With the whole Apollo programme costing $US 25 billion, a portion of Moon rock works out at $US 66 million a kilogram!

Watched by millions of television viewers, Armstrong and Aldrin spent 2½ hours gathering rock and soil samples. The footprints they left behind them will still be there 10 million years from now.

MOON LANDING
Once Apollo was in orbit around the Moon, one astronaut stayed in the CSM while the other two moved into the LM. The LM separated from the CSM (4) and descended to the Moon (5).

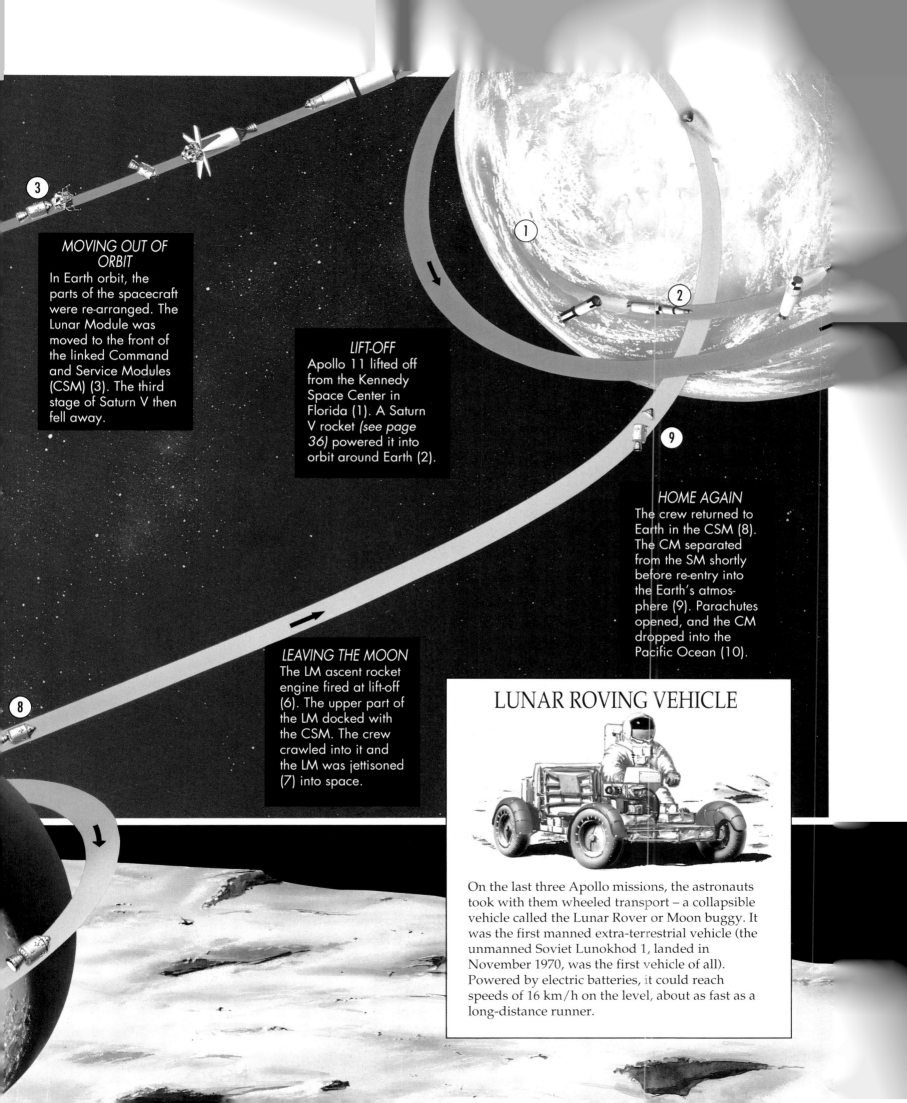

MOVING OUT OF ORBIT
In Earth orbit, the parts of the spacecraft were re-arranged. The Lunar Module was moved to the front of the linked Command and Service Modules (CSM) (3). The third stage of Saturn V then fell away.

LIFT-OFF
Apollo 11 lifted off from the Kennedy Space Center in Florida (1). A Saturn V rocket *(see page 36)* powered it into orbit around Earth (2).

HOME AGAIN
The crew returned to Earth in the CSM (8). The CM separated from the SM shortly before re-entry into the Earth's atmosphere (9). Parachutes opened, and the CM dropped into the Pacific Ocean (10).

LEAVING THE MOON
The LM ascent rocket engine fired at lift-off (6). The upper part of the LM docked with the CSM. The crew crawled into it and the LM was jettisoned (7) into space.

LUNAR ROVING VEHICLE

On the last three Apollo missions, the astronauts took with them wheeled transport – a collapsible vehicle called the Lunar Rover or Moon buggy. It was the first manned extra-terrestrial vehicle (the unmanned Soviet Lunokhod 1, landed in November 1970, was the first vehicle of all). Powered by electric batteries, it could reach speeds of 16 km/h on the level, about as fast as a long-distance runner.

HIGH FLYERS

HIGH ALTITUDE RECORD HOLDERS

MANY OF THE STARS we see in the sky are so far away we have to measure their distances in light-years. One light-year is the distance travelled by light, moving at 299,792 kilometres per second, in one year – that is, more than 9 million million kilometres. Even the nearest star (apart from the Sun) is more than 4 light-years away. The farthest object ever detected may be more than 13 *billion* light-years distant!

By comparison, the greatest efforts made by humans to lift themselves clear of their home planet are humble indeed. The altitude record is held by the crew of Apollo 13, whose spacecraft reached a distance of just over 400,000 kilometres from the Earth on 15 April 1970. It was, however, a major advance over the first ever manned space flight made by Yuri Gagarin, whose *Vostok I* spacecraft climbed to an altitude of 327 kilometres just nine years earlier.

Apart from spacecraft, the champion high-flyer is the US rocket-powered plane X-15, also famous for its speed records (*see page 33*). It could fly so high – more than 100,000 metres – its pilot was able to qualify as an astronaut! Jet-powered planes cannot ascend to such heights because they need air for their engines to work. A MiG fighter jet holds the altitude record at 37,650 metres.

HIGHEST IN A BALLOON

The greatest height ever reached by a manned balloon is 37,735 m, achieved by Nicholas Piantanida in South Dakota in February 1966. Unfortunately, Piantanida did not survive the feat and his achievement is not recognized as a record. The official altitude record is therefore still held by US Navy officers Malcolm Ross and Victor Prather, whose elongated balloon *Lee Lewis Memorial* lifted them to 34,668 m above the Gulf of Mexico in 1961.

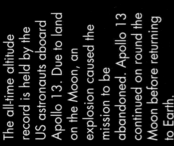

The all-time altitude record is held by the US astronauts aboard Apollo 13. Due to land on the Moon, an explosion caused the mission to be abandoned. Apollo 13 continued on round the Moon before returning to Earth.

MOON 384,400 km

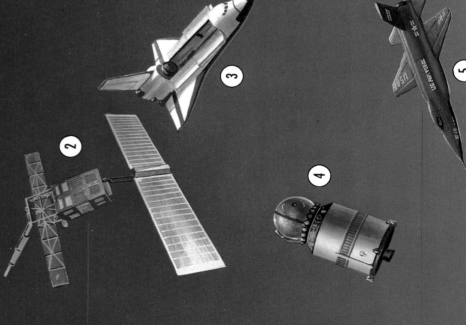

MT. EVEREST *Highest mountain* 8863 m

KEY

1 Apollo 13 *Farthest manned flight* 15 April 1970 400,187 km
2 Satellite 36,000 km
3 Space Shuttle
4 Vostok 1 *First manned space flight* 12 April 1961 327 km
5 X-15 *Highest flight by aircraft* 22 August 1963 107,960 m
6 MiG 25 *Highest flight by jet aircraft* 31 August 1977 37,650 m
7 Lee Lewis Memorial *Highest flight by balloon* 4 May 1961 34,668 m
8 Lockheed SR-71 Blackbird 30,000 m
9 Concorde 18,000 m
10 Aérospatiale SA315b Lama *Highest flight by helicopter*
  12 June 1972 12,442 m
11 Boeing 747 10,000 m

The illustrations are not drawn to scale

HUBBLE SPACE TELESCOPE
GIANT STAR-WATCHER IN ORBIT

THE BEST TELESCOPES in the world all suffer from one thing: the air they must 'see' through is polluted and tends to move about. Because of this, more distant stars appear faint or blurred, even if observatories are sited (as many are) on mountaintops far away from city lights and smog. So the best-performing telescopes would have to be located above the Earth's atmosphere. That is exactly where the most powerful of them all, the Hubble Space Telescope, is to be found – orbiting 616 kilometres above the Earth.

Like most modern large telescopes, the Hubble is a reflector: it uses mirrors to focus an image of the stars or galaxies it is pointed towards. Now, astronomers are able to see clearly stars 50 times fainter and 10 times farther away than they could using any of the best telescopes on the ground. The Hubble Space Telescope is so powerful it could detect light from a tiny flashlight over 400,000 kilometres away.

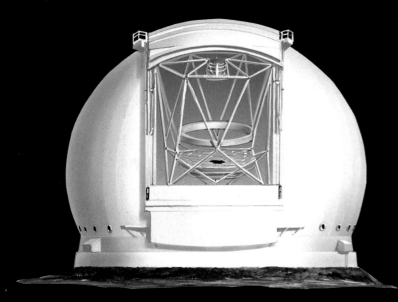

THE HONEYCOMB TELESCOPE

The Keck telescope, sitting atop the 4200-m peak of Mauna Kea on Hawaii, is the world's largest telescope. Its light-collecting mirror, measuring 10 m across, consists of 36 hexagons fitted together in a honeycomb pattern. This is almost twice as large as a mirror in the world's next best telescope, the 508-cm Hale telescope at Mount Palomar, California. (The largest single-mirror instrument, on Mount Semirodriki, Russia, is not in a good observing site.) The Keck telescope is so sensitive that it could detect a candle shining more than 100,000 km away!

INSIDE THE HUBBLE
The main mirror (1) reflects light from distant stars and galaxies on to the secondary mirror (2). This focuses the light down through a central tube (3) to detectors (4). A television image can be transmitted down to Earth using the antennae (5). Computers are used to re-direct the telescope. Solar panels (6) turn sunlight into electric power for the telescope.

person to gaze at the night sky through a telescope. To his amazement, he saw that the Moon had mountains and craters, and that the planet Jupiter had several moons circling around it. He also discovered many new stars, never before seen by humans.

THE RACE OF THE RECORD HOLDERS

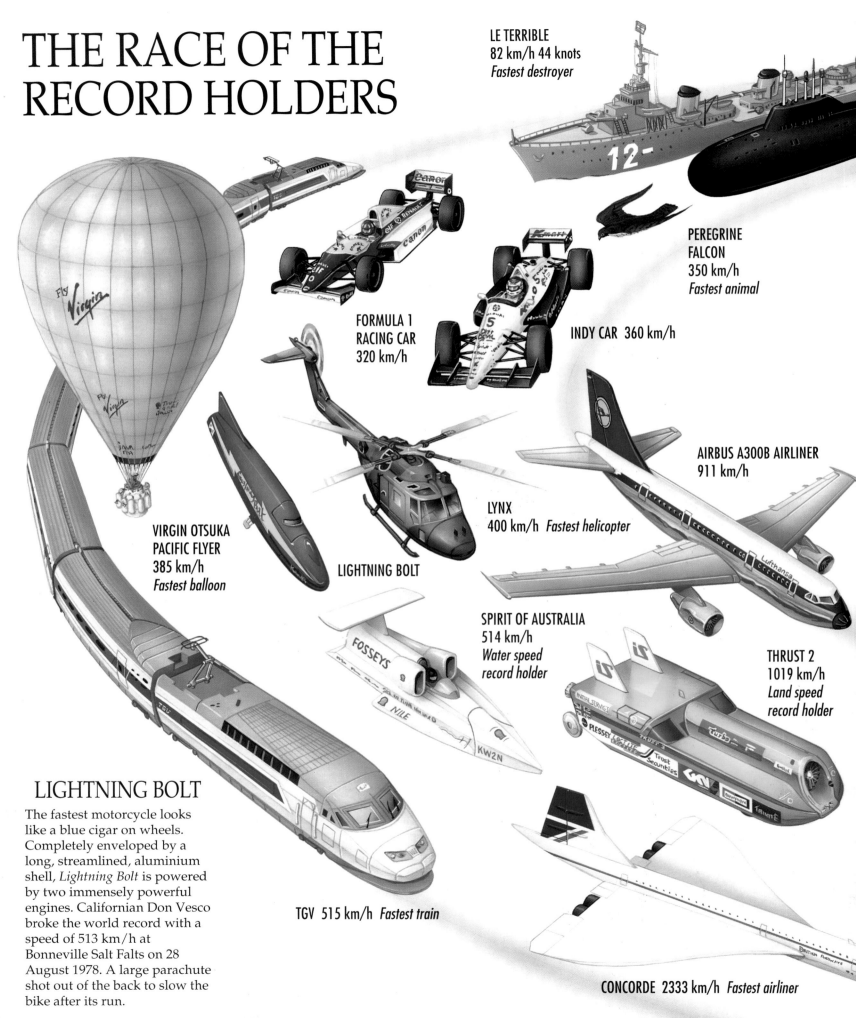

LE TERRIBLE
82 km/h 44 knots
Fastest destroyer

PEREGRINE FALCON
350 km/h
Fastest animal

FORMULA 1 RACING CAR
320 km/h

INDY CAR 360 km/h

AIRBUS A300B AIRLINER
911 km/h

LYNX
400 km/h *Fastest helicopter*

VIRGIN OTSUKA PACIFIC FLYER
385 km/h
Fastest balloon

LIGHTNING BOLT

SPIRIT OF AUSTRALIA
514 km/h
Water speed record holder

THRUST 2
1019 km/h
Land speed record holder

LIGHTNING BOLT

The fastest motorcycle looks like a blue cigar on wheels. Completely enveloped by a long, streamlined, aluminium shell, *Lightning Bolt* is powered by two immensely powerful engines. Californian Don Vesco broke the world record with a speed of 513 km/h at Bonneville Salt Falts on 28 August 1978. A large parachute shot out of the back to slow the bike after its run.

TGV 515 km/h *Fastest train*

CONCORDE 2333 km/h *Fastest airliner*

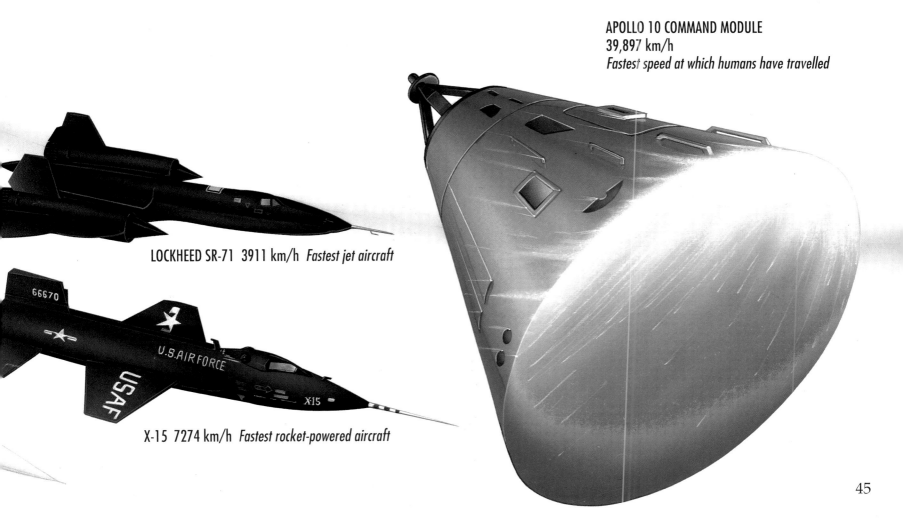

RACING BICYCLE 72 km/h

RACEHORSE 69 km/h

UNITED STATES
66 km/h 36 knots
Fastest ocean liner

J CLASS RACING YACHT 56 km/h 30 knots

THERMOPYLAE 39 km/h
One of the fastest clippers

ALFA CLASS SUBMARINE
82 km/h 44 knots *Fastest submarine*

THE GREATEST SPEEDS achieved by manmade machines have all been reached in space, where there is no air to slow an object down. Even a satellite orbits the Earth at twice the speed of the fastest aircraft. An unmanned space probe Helios B sent to observe the Sun holds the all-time speed record of 252,800 km/h. A spacecraft moving at that speed it would travel from the Earth to the Moon in an hour and a half! The crew of Apollo 10, US astronauts Thomas Stafford, Eugene Cernan and John Young, hold the record for the fastest speed at which humans have travelled, when their command module returned from the Moon on 26 May 1969.

The illustrations are not drawn to scale

One hundred and fifty years ago, large sailing ships called clippers *(above)* vied with each other to be the quickest on the high seas. Loaded with tea and powered only by the wind, the clippers raced non-stop from China to Europe – more than halfway around the world – in about 100 days. But, apart from watercraft specially designed to break records, sea-going speed champions are well down the field when it comes to compare their speeds with others. A clipper never went faster than a human sprinter, and both a modern racing yacht and the fastest ocean liner (the *United States*) would be comfortably left behind by a racehorse. Only the quickest warships and submarines would outpace a racing cyclist, but any family car could easily overtake them all.

APOLLO 10 COMMAND MODULE
39,897 km/h
Fastest speed at which humans have travelled

LOCKHEED SR-71 3911 km/h *Fastest jet aircraft*

X-15 7274 km/h *Fastest rocket-powered aircraft*

INDEX